SAILING THROUGH LIFE ON

THE HIGH SEAS

BY

ROBERT H DUNHAM

PROLOGUE

This story is about a man who has traveled the world and – by God's grace –made it back.

COUNTRIES:

North America:

Canada

Mexico

Belize

Baha Peninsula

Puerto Rico

St. Thomas

USA – all 50 states and Washington, D.C.

Traveling by car, heavy duty truck, bus, taxi, foot, plane, cruise and ships.

South America

Aruba

Bolivia

Chili

Venezuela

Equator

Columbia

Peru

Panama (via cruise)

Europe

England

Spain

France

Italy

Netherlands

Holland

Belgium

Africa

Egypt

Liberia

The Orient

Japan

Taiwan

Korea

Vietnam

Philippine Islands

Travels by: Ocean freighters, Naval Ships, Oil Tankers, planes, bus, taxi, cars, rickshaws.

Now, I am retired, a property owner of Franklin, North Carolina. At 80, married to the same woman for over 56 years and counting.

God has blessed me beyond measure – and He continues to do this. Hope you enjoy my life's adventures.

Bob,

DEDICATION

ACKNOWLEDGEMENT

I thank my wife for all her assistance in editing, typing, and inspiring me.

Also, Nick, my new friend and publisher.

God bless you both.

Bob

TABLE OF CONTENTS

CHAPTER 1:

EARLY LIFE IN TUSCALOOSA

I was born in Tuscaloosa, Alabama on the 4th of July 1944. A time when the world was at war and the American South ticked at a much slower pace. Tuscaloosa, with its oak- lined streets and the distant hum of the Black Warrior River, was a tight-knit community where the neighbors knew each other by name and the University of Alabama's Crimson Tide brought the community together. My family, the Dunham's, were anchored to this lovely Southern town, and the love, discipline and faith that formed my childhood.

My first years were spent in a Tuscaloosa that was both old and "on the move". A place that was both infused with old traditions of the old South and the swirl of World War II. The town was a combination of humble houses, busy downtown stores, and the ever-peent paper mill, whose acrid odor would float in the air if the wind blew at the right moment. It wasn't a nice smell, but it was part of fabric of our town....a smell that reminded us the it was that industry that kept the town humming.

My first memories are a swirl of sights and sounds of Tuscaloosa. I can recall standing at the corner two blocks from our home and watching the Alabama football homecoming parade going by. The air was filled with excitement when floats from fraternity and sorority houses decorated with crape paper and with bold slogans such as "**Alabama beat Auburn**" made their way down the street. The University of Alabama band played, even the bands of the local high schools participated, and the cheerleaders threw candy to us kids and our eyes were wide with awe. To an eight-year-old, it was a show as big as a circus, an annual ritual that stitched the town together in Crimson Tide unity. The Alabama Crimson Tide was not just a team, it was a part of the town's spirit, and supporting them was a rite of passage. We were taught to be patriotic, to respect the sacrifices of men, such as my father, who went to war so we could be free, and be proud to be an American. Politically our family was Republican, which reflected my father's individual beliefs, but also his belief in small government.

The noises of our neighborhood were also very noticeable, the noise of a car horn blowing, the sound of a dog barking, or the distant sound of a bicycle clattering down the street. I was born into a family of hardcore values and Southern grit. My father was an ensign in the Naval service in the South Pacific until the end of World War II. He made it back home in 1945. He patriotically joined the Alabama National Guard as a Captain of infantry after he returned home. Then President Truman sent his "Dixie Division" portion of the National Guard to Korea in 1951, after being home for only six years since the last war. After three months in Korea, however, he was sent home, because of a loophole found by a clever sergeant Dad worked with, "because he had already served time in World War II he could go home immediately." God was looking after our family.

His absence had created a vacuum in our life, but also a feeling of pride that we all wore as a badge. My mother, who was a college graduate and former teacher, was the rock in our home. She was a college educator for women's sports before her marriage, but the "norms" of the time made her leave her work as educator after she got married. She then poured her intellect and energy into raising her sons, giving us a strong sense of right and wrong as well as a deep faith in God.

Our family grew with the birth of my brother, Joe, in March of 1949. My older brother Bill was my comrade-in-mischief and adventure. Joe unfortunately became an object of our teasing. The three of us were a trio of boys experiencing the thrills and bumps of childhood in a world not polluted with the distractions of modern technology. There were no private telephones or cell phones, but only a party line that had characteristic rings for each household. For instance, our ring was a sharp "bing bing", the neighbor's might be 3 "bings". Privacy was an issue of mutual consideration, you were not to eavesdrop – unless you wanted a lecture from you parents. There was no television – radio was our link to the world, bringing classical music to our living room, as well as the adventures of the Lone Ranger, or tales of The Shadow.

The Dunham household was a little republic, with our father as the head, our mother as the heart. When my father was around, his authority was never called into question, but his quiet kindness made him a hero for us. He was a man of principle, who was molded by his days in the military and his desire to support his family. My mother, who was no longer teaching professionally, was a teacher in all aspects to us. She ran our home with dignity and strictness, making sure that we went to Sunday school and Church every Sunday, behaved properly, and learned "the Golden Rule": "Treat other people the same way you would like them to treat you". Her Baptist faith was the underpinning of our childhood, and she practiced it every day, imparting to us the values of kindness and humility helping to make us good Christians and good citizens. Her influence on all of us was strong. Her mind and faith had taken us through the uncertainties of war. Her teachings were timeless and eternal: be polite, be honest. Her educator's spirit never died even after she had left teaching. She was our first teacher, telling us what was right and wrong and preparing us for the world outside of Tuscaloosa.

My mother had to take care of three boys while my father was away during wartime. She was our disciplinarian, our storyteller, our moral compass. When my father came back home from Korea our family was complete again. His presence meant stability and a re-invigoration of adventure. We got to go fishing, hunting at the storied Dollarhide Hunt Club in West Alabama, and came to know the rhythms of a Southern man's life.

My brothers and I were inseparable, united by the commonalities of boyhood, whether playing hide-and-seek or playing baseball. My brothers and I enjoyed playing all manner of "made-up" games. On one unfortunate occasion I tied a sheet around my neck to play Superman, jumping eight steps off the back porch only to land on a rock in the back yard, and broke my arm. This was the time when lessons came hard and fast, and sometimes painful, but always with love and support. Sadly, I still can't fly. Children were free to roam, to fantasize and learn by being clumsy – like when I realized I couldn't fly!

Life at home was simpler, but no less wonderful. My brothers and I enjoyed playing and a good dare. One time, in a moment of madness, Bill bet me that I wouldn't run around the block Buck naked. He lost. However, I was met with the wrath of my parents who found it much less amusing than I did. Another time we spun the neighbor's cat by its tail, a thing we were **very** sorry for when our parents caught us and stopped the nonsense. These were the mistakes of youth, chastened by the advice of a family, which guided us to do better. From the perspective of time, my childhood in Tuscaloosa was idyllic. A strong sense of being loved. It was a time when life was not such a rush, where family sat down to dinner every night, and prayed. The values of faith, respect and patriotism were instilled in me and became the cornerstones of my life. These early years, parades, life lessons, and times of excitement are at the very heart of my story.

Our home had faith in America. We were Baptists, Sundays were sanctified with church, Sunday School, hymns, sermons, and comradeship. The dedication of my mother to Christianity influenced our moral system, where we learned to trust in God's purpose and live with compassion. We also had a strong sense of community in our cultural upbringing.

Chapter 2:

Southern Childhood and Moves

In 1951, my family experienced a great change when we moved from Tuscaloosa, Alabama to Columbia, South Carolina. I was Robert H. Dunham and at that time I was a little boy, aged eight years old, living with the uncertainties of this move. The troubles and the thoughts that my father, an officer, could be sent to war, cast a shadow over my family. This wasn't an adventure or a business opportunity sort of move, it was necessity of duty. The weight of it was palatable. The circumstances under which we moved were not a happy one. My father's National Guard unit, the "Dixie Division", had been mobilized for war training to prepare for the Korean war. When we arrived in South Carolina, we moved into an apartment just outside of Columbia, a benefit of my father being an officer. The adjustment was challenging. The tense atmosphere was created by the military environment and the permanent awareness of the possible deployment of my father. Children, however, are resilient. My brothers and I managed to adjust to the 4th grade (Bill), 3rd grade (me) respectively, in a new school, in a new state, which had its own challenges with new routines, new classmates, and a new life.

One of the most striking memories from this period was a small moment of excitement in all this uncertainty. My father, as any loving parent might do, took Bill and I to the army training grounds. There we got the unforgettable experience of traveling in a Sherman tank. For an eight-year-old, the roar of the tank and the excitement of going round the lot was as magical as it gets. It was a short respite from the pervading terror that our father could be called upon to fight in war any time soon. These were moments of joy, that were priceless, and held us together as we struggled with the emotional complexity.

The neighborhood children, my brothers, and I found relief in play. With the Korean war in the back of our minds, our game were always, as a rule, war games. We didn't pretend to be superheroes, such as Superman or Batman, but soldiers fighting communists, Nazis, or another enemy. A construction site that was close to our home, where condos were being built, became our playground. Mountains of logs and lumber became forts or tanks in our creative wars. We even found that huge cardboard boxes could be used as improvised tanks for us to crawl across the field until an unforeseen hill knocked us off. These games, which were innocent, captured the tensions of the time, viewed through the prism of childhood

Once my brothers and I adapted to life in South Carolina, we looked for opportunities to show our independence. My brothers and I talked our Dad into buying us a power lawn mower, a new item in the neighborhood. We saved our allowances and started cutting our neighbor's lawns for spending money – additionally it provided an enormous sense of achievement. This entrepreneurial mindset was a small step forward to self-reliance, which made us feel more at home in our new environment.

Fortunately, faith in the Lord saved us from the calamity that we had feared – Dad came home. Our family packed again and moved back to Alabama – not to Tuscaloosa – but to

Birmingham, the big Steel City – where new adventures lay. The relocation to Birmingham was a boon for our family. Relocation to South Carolina and the return to Birmingham were life-defining moments in my early life. I was also a new beginning for our family, my father joined Dunham GMC Trucking Company, a family business that was co-owned by my Grandfather, my Dad and his older brother. The company traded in GMC trucks and later expanded its scope of franchises to include that of Keiser Jeeps, Peterbilt Trucks, and Mercedes Benz Trucks. The career of my father in the automotive industry settled in, so there was stability after the turmoil of South Carolina – and Korea.

In Birmingham, I joined the third grade and Bill joined fourth grade at Shades Cahaba Grammar School. South Carolina schools were not as rigorous as Brimingham's Shades Cahaba Grammar School. The move to Birmingham schools necessitated me making an academic effort – and social efforts, in order to make new friends. The school was more organized, the teachers demanded more from us, we realized that we were no longer "little kids". This change in expectations helped me develop, but I soon realized that I lacked any musical talent, I simply could NOT read music. My brief experiments with the violin and drums were not to the satisfaction of my parents who had purchased the musical instruments. The only music I could play was on the radio – Although I loved music, I couldn't play any instruments, so my musical career was over before it started. I began to accept this shortcoming in my life.

Bill, the most athletic among us, was great at football, and he soon attracted the attention of coaches as an excellent quarterback. The fame Bill created for himself at Shades Cahaba lead to an unusual event. A new student came to school when Bill was in the 8th grade. He found it hard to make friends and to fit in. His solution was to challenge Bill Dunham, the most well-known, kid in the school to a fight after classes the next day. His world changed. Kids in his class began to speak to him, girls noticed him and were friendly. Who would want to fight Bill? The next day after school, the buses had to run late because most of the students were going to the playground to wait for the big fight. Me too. The bell rang, everyone ran out of the building and gathered around. The opponents met. It was obvious the new young man didn't stand a chance. He stood his ground as Bill approached. Face to face, Bill said *"I admire your courage. A fight isn't necessary. Let's be friends"*, and extended his hand to the shock of his new friend. But the boy took Bill's hand and everyone cheered, the principal breathed a sigh of relief, and everyone went home admiring both opponents.

I did not fare as well as an athlete. During my sophomore year in high school, I had to cut my football career short after I broke my leg during spring training. The injury was a big blow and required a week in the hospital and months on crutches, duly attended to by my brother Joe. The 12-pound cast was not only heavy, but unwieldy and the agony of getting up on crutches was humbling. But, my family supported me – my younger brother, Joe, even carried my leg to help avoid the cast hitting the ground during the early stages of recovery. Support from my family, coupled with things like moving my bedroom nearer to the bathroom, made the recovery bearable. Nevertheless, the injury put an end to my athletic ambitions, and I had to divert my efforts to something else.

New friendships were a result of the move to Birmingham. My best friend, Ralph, lived across the street. We became very good friends by doing things together, like earning the rank of Eagle Scout at the same time. Both families doing things together. We worshipped together and my antics in the balcony during services caused me great troubles with the deacons. With time, we grew up, and Ralph is a lifelong friend – even when our paths separated us – me to the Merchant Marine Academy and Ralph to Tulane University toward becoming a doctor. Getting together with him years later near Mobile, Alabama in 2015, was a fun way to remember our past together in high school in a fun and nostalgic way.

The constant moving and the constant fear of my father getting deployed during the Korean War influenced my childhood. All moves meant having to make new friends and finding oneself in "foreign surroundings". Being a member of the Boy Scouts was my way of shining. Rather than Bill, who was focused on athletics, I got immersed in scouting and ultimately became an Eagle Scout and a camp counselor. Scouting provided discipline and camaraderie and my induction into the Order of the Arrow made me feel that I had achieved something.

Faith was important in my upbringing, particularly after we moved back to Birmingham. Although we went to church occasionally, we were moving, until putting down roots in Birmingham. Dawson Memorial Baptist Church became our spiritual home. My parents were very faithful and made sure that my brothers and I went to Sunday School and services as often as possible. As a young boy I loved the stories and the teachings of the Bible, but I didn't really become religious until my early teens. After my thirteenth birthday, my father invited our pastor to our home. Bill and I listened as the pastor spoke about the importance of accepting Christ and trusting Him as Savior to properly live our lives. The message touched the very depths of our souls. Bill and I made our decisions to accept Christ and His finished work on the cross for us as our Savior. A few weeks later Bill and I were baptized. This achievement was not just a ritual, but a promise to live with a purpose and integrity for Jesus.

Church became a part of my life, despite the boundaries I tested with my friend John, in the balcony. The deacons' kind hand served as our guidance to maturity and by the time we reached high school, I was more involved in the church community. My faith gave me a moral compass through which I could better overcome the challenges of growing up, peer pressure, and college preparation. Although my stay at the Merchant Marine Academy took me away from church attendance, the foundation laid at Dawson Memorial Baptist Church was a leading force in my life.

I guess the biggest challenge was planning for my future. Having been inspired by the television series "Men of Annapolis", I dreamed of going to the Naval Academy. When that door was shut, I applied to the United States Merchant Marine Academy at Kings Point, New York. The application process was exhaustive and I was put on the "wait list" as number nine out of six slots for Alabama. After some persistence and lucky dropouts, I got a place at the Academy ten days before the beginning of the term. This change was a starting point for my career as a merchant marine officer.

These challenges taught me resilience, adaptability, and the importance of family. My injury, finding my place, and pursuing my dreams made my character, while the faith remained an unwavering anchor. From riding in a Sherman tank to my Eagle Scout badge, from breaking my leg to my acceptance to Kings Point, all of it made me the man I am. My reunion with my father after the Korean War is still one of the happiest moments of my life. Evidence of the strength of family ties that withstand time. Looking back at these years, I am thankful for what I learned and the faith that supported me through it all.

"Dunham GMC/Peterbilt Trucks" needed a person who could work with a computer to be their Warranty Manager. I quickly asked for the job even though it was a complete departure from my nautical training. The interview with my Uncle was successful, I thought. The job was challenging, but I mastered it. My first paycheck was a huge disappointment. Instead of the $650/month I thought my Uncle and I agreed to, it was only $500/month. The Service Manager and I shared an office, and I ran the computer. By the end of the year, Peterbilt was thinking of pulling the franchise from *Dunham GMC* unless they did a better job in the next six months. They hired a "Make-

over Specialist" to help them fix the problems. One of his immediate recommendations was to change the Parts Manager from the current one to me. My Uncle and Dad agreed. A raise to $950/month. By the end of the year I had turned the parts sales around to over $100,000 per month from $50,000 a month. In fact, we won a contest from Peterbilt that took both the Service Manager, his wife, Janie and myself to Hawaii for an all expenses paid week of fun in the sun. No raise, but they treated me much better.

My Uncle thought the company was losing thousands of dollars a year to theft. The first inventory I ran with computers, the employees of al departments helped us count. The ending value of all parts was within a dollar of what the book said we had. No loss to theft.

Six months later we counted everything again, and matched the book value within the cost of a cigarette lighter. This, in addition to the fact that we increased Parts Sales to $100,000 or better each month and the size of the inventory by better than $60,000, all accounted for on my computer. Such a turnaround helped the Service Department improve, also, by having the correct parts stock instead of waiting for the factory to ship it to us. This made the customers happy and told their friends and everyone was happy. Still no raise for me. Peterbilt, however, was so impressed - they called me with an offer to work for them at their factory (parts sales division) in Nashville, Tennessee, for $1,450/month plus expenses for traveling. It was a happy occasion when I was able to submit my letter of resignation to my Uncle.

Janie and I moved to the Nashville area, (Ridgetop, Tennessee) to a great salt-box style home with 3 bedrooms and two baths, kitchen and dining room and a large family room with a fireplace. It had a laundry room in the breezeway between the house and the two car garage. My job was to travel through the Midwest to each Peterbilt Parts Store at their various dealerships, visit a few days and report back to the factory. I trained new employees, checked on inventory control, warranty submissions, you name it, I did it. Everything concerning the various parts departments. I would work one week at the factory in Nashville, and one week in the field. I would come home, plan the next trip, write up my notes and recommendations for the dealerships I had just visited. This was an excellent opportunity to learn the trucking business.

Chapter 3:

Education and Merchant Marine

My dream of attending the United States Naval Academy began in high school. It wasn't a career counselor or a recruiter who sparked that dream, it was a television show which did it for me. It was shows like **Men of Annapolis** and **West Point** that played once a week on television that stirred something inside me. My older brother Bill had earned a football scholarship to VMI (Virginia Military Academy), an Army college. I chose the Navy as my professional career. At the time, the Merchant Marine Academy wasn't even on my radar, I had my eyes on the Naval Academy.

When senior year came and it was time to apply for college, I submitted my application to the United States Naval Academy. It was my high school counselor who suggested the Merchant Marine Academy as an alternative for me. He explained what it was, what it taught, and how it might be a good fit for me. I applied to the United States Merchant Marine Academy at Kings Point, New York. The Naval Academy turned me down, but the Merchant Marine Academy placed me on their waitlist as number nine out of six available slots for Alabama.

With that uncertainty hanging over me, I made other plans. I applied to the University to Alabama and participated in their fraternity "rush" weekends. Since my father and uncle had both been Kappa Sigma's, I visited their house and was welcomed warmly. While I was there, I met a young lady who asked if I had heard of the Merchant Marine Academy. I told her I was trying to get in. She casually mentioned that her boyfriend had given up his spot, which bumped me up from number nine to number eight.

Later during that same evening, I spoke with another girl whose boyfriend had failed his physical exam. That moved me to number seven. Much later, I learned that the sixth candidate had gotten his girlfriend pregnant and decided to stay home and get married. Just like that, I became number six and had my spot!

Soon after, I got a call from Kings Point. The phone rang and my father answered it. He handed me the receiver with a smile: *"They want to know if you can be in New York in ten days"* and I said *"yes"* without any hesitation.

After receiving my orders to report to The Merchant Marine Academy, I spent the last night before departing for New York with my long-time girlfriend, Sherry. We promised each other we would be faithful for the next four years. This didn't last a year on either side.

Boarding the plane in Birmingham and landing at LaGuardia Airport in New York marked only the second time I had traveled by airplane. My parents had given me directions, $50.00 and a change of clothes. From LaGuardia Airport, I took a cab to Penn Station and caught a train to Great Neck, and finally a bus to the Academy, along with other incoming cadets. It was the beginning of a new adventure – Plebe year had begun.

Kings Point was a place of strict order and structure. The Regiment was divided into three battalions, six companies, twelve platoons and 36 squads. The seniors, as first classmen, ran the show, and as a fourth-classman, or plebe, I was trained by selected sophomores. We learned everything from how to salute properly, and how to dress in uniform, and how to make a bed! That two week introduction, known as the Prep Period, was difficult for me. Out of 350 candidates who were there, more than seventy-five dropped out, but I stayed to fulfill my dreams in the US Maritime Service.

Once classes began, life settled into a rigid routine. Wake-up was 6 a.m. in the morning, followed by inspection at 6:30, breakfast at 7, followed by morning naval uniform inspection and formal march called Colors. We marched around the flag pole and then went to class. Demerits were handed out for any violations in grooming, dress, or behavior. Ten demerits meant losing Saturday liberty (ability to leave Academy grounds). I had 183 demerits during my first year. One of my classmates accumulated more than 2,000 and was dismissed.

Under constant scrutiny as Plebes, we longed for more freedom, which finally came during our second year. In early September, I received orders to ship out for my "Sea Year" as a sophomore. My first assignment was aboard the SS Dolly Turman, a World War II-era Lyke Brothers transport ship. We sailed for the Mediterranean, visiting Barcelona, Spain. Barcelona was our first foreign country. What excitement! The engine cadet and I (a Deck Cadet) set out to explore a new city in a new country on a new continent!. Neither of us spoke

Spanish and we walked around in the crowded city not understanding a word or able to read a sign – it was a bit discouraging. Then we heard two young women, our age, speaking English. We joined forces and spent a wonderful day exploring the city with two lovely ladies from Canada.

Then on to Marseille, France. We tied up after dark too late to go ashore. Bright and early the following morning we went into Marseille. Unfortunately, the French people resented Americans and were unwaveringly "rude". After a few hours of recurring, constant distain, we returned to the ship to leave France behind. From France we went to West Germany (at the time, Germany was still divided between East and West Germany), to the city of Bremerhaven. We unloaded, allowing only a very short shore visit. We did meet a couple of very nice German young people who were very kind to us.

Then on to Rome, Italy. The Captain took the other Cadet and me on a tour of Rome, the Sistine Chapel, the Colosseum, and other wonders I had only read about. From there, we visited Pompeii then on to Venice, a floating city of canals and pigeons. We had a brief stop in Libya, which left more sensory memories than cultural ones. In Alexandria, Egypt, I stood before the Great Pyramids and the Sphinx, awed by the ancient artifacts of that civilization.

This took 3 ½ months of my Sea Year. I returned to Birmingham, Alabama for Christmas leave. Took Ralph's younger sister to see the first James Bond 007 movie, and what a surprise, sitting behind us were the young folks I had met in Germany. Life is full of surprises.

My next journey was on the SS Leslie Lykes, and headed to Antwerp, Belgium where we unloaded general freight, and then on to the Rotterdam, Netherlands. It was the middle of a **very** cold winter. We sailed from the pier into the canal that led to the Atlantic Ocean. The weather turned even colder and the canal froze and we were trapped in the ice. The ship trapped with us was a Russian freighter. The crew was friendly and invited us over for coffee and vodka. One of the crew took us on a tour of his ship. When the canal thawed, we sailed for England. After we docked in England in 1962, my fellow cadet and I went ashore and we met a pair of local girls who invited us to a Beatles concert. We eagerly accepted, but before the night came, the ship's whistle blew. An English dockworker's strike meant we had to leave port immediately. We missed the show. At the time, however, we didn't realize how iconic the Beatles would become. That missed concert remains one of my greatest regrets.

The next Lykes ship, SS Doctor Lykes, was a larger ship. We sailed the "Doctor" through the Panama canal toward

Japan. We sailed right by Hawaii and two months later docked in Yokohama, Japan. Japan is a beautiful country. The natives treated us wonderfully. I thoroughly enjoyed myself. After unloading our cargo, we sailed for Pusan, Korea, where we unloaded more cargo and then on to Incheon, Korea where we ran into some **very, very, extreme** cold. Our next port of call was Taipei, Formosa. Taipei, brought a number of new experiences to my life. Then on to Saigon, Vietnam. The French were gone and the American Army wasn't there yet. Saigon was not yet embroiled in war and retained its sleepy French charm. While anchored in Da Nang, Vietnam, a group of us rented a jeep and drove up the now infamous Highway 1, unknowingly crossing into North Vietnam. Armed soldiers stopped us and ordered us to turn back. We didn't slow down until we were back on the ship. You can't fix stupid! God was watching over us.

While in Saigon, the first engineer asked the Engineering Cadet (Nate) and I (a Deck Cadet) to go ashore and purchase bicycles for his children. We had his permission, and his money, so we walked to a shop and purchased two bikes. We leisurely rode back to the ship and brought the bikes aboard. The First Engineer was delighted, but when the Chief Engineer saw us returning from shore, he lost his temper (he had previously told the Engineering Cadet he was confined to ship). He ran into our cabin and physically attacked the Engineering Cadet, just short of striking him. The First Engineer managed to calm him down. He would have lost his livelihood if the First Engineer hadn't been able to stop him. The Captain investigated, but asked us to "keep the event on board" and did not report the incident to the Coast Guard. From that point on we were treated like royalty. Later in Taipei, Formosa, we had a memorable night out. We went by rikshaw to a local bar. We walked in behind two Swedish Sailors who picked up two local girls. When the local girls realized we were Americans, they left the Swedes and joined our group. The Chief Engineer paid for everything! The next day we rejoined the girls and they showed us their city. Before heading home, we stopped in Manila, Philippines. After discharging the last of our cargo, we anchored at a small island to load mahogany (wood used in making furniture). While loading we all went ashore. We ordered fried chicken at the only restaurant on the island. It was really the only thing on the menu so we ordered chicken. Shortly after ordering the chicken, we saw the owner running after free-range chickens – we knew our meal would be fresh! Our trip to the Orient was over when we sailed for home.

My fourth ship was the SS Gulf Banker. The Captain and many of his crew had been on board this ship for a very long time. We visited the Panama Canal, Bolivia, Columbia, Ecuador, Peru, and we finally reached our las port of call, Valparaiso, Chile. In Chile, the Captain gave an enormous party and invited every party girl in town. It was an unforgettable celebration for the entire crew as the ship was to be sold for scrap when we got back to the U.S.A. On the trip home from South America, the Captain and I were talking. The Captain mentioned he had sailed for the U.S. Navy in the South Pacific theater. So had my father, I said, on a little ship the APC #45. The Captain looked at me in surprise. *"That was my ship. I was scheduled to be relieved as soon as my replacement arrived. As I walked to the end of the pier and ashore, my replacement saluted me as we passed and I was on my way home. That man on the pier was your father!"* What a coincidence!. While my son "Chris" was at the USMMA, class of 2001, he wrote an English paper about this incident in the South Pacific. He passed English, needless to say. Graduated in 2001 and began working for GE Nuclear Division. He still works in the nuclear field as an Engineer for Southern Company at one of their nuclear plants, in Vidalia, Georgia.

When I returned to New Orleans, I received orders to board another Lykes ship in Mobile. With my 20th birthday just around the corner, I wanted to go home. But orders are orders. While boarding, I twisted my ankle badly. An ambulance took me a local hospital. My parents kindly drove down from

Birmingham to take me home for the rest of the summer. I reported back to Kings Point in September, 1964, having sailed all over the world at a time America was respected, if not loved. The U.S. dollar was the world's currency. You could spend a $20.00 bill anywhere in the world.

Sea year taught me more about life, leadership, risk, and culture than I ever imagined. After my wonderful sea year and my trips all over the world, I reported back to Kings Point in the fall of 1964 as a second classman, which was far easier than Plebe year. We had earned respect, and our weekends in New York were a reward. We could leave school Friday, after classes and stay out until Sunday, at 4:30 pm. One weekend, some friends and I met with a few kind girls from Detroit, they allowed us to sleep in their hotel room while they went shopping. When they returned, they found eight cadets sprawling across the floor. No cadet could afford a hotel room in New York! Academics were tough but manageable.

In my final year, as a First Classman (seniors), was the best year of the three spent on campus. We were now the class in charge. The Cadet Officers came from our ranks. I had previously joined the Academy Drill Team as a Second Classman, but I took on leadership role and became the Senior Chief Petty Officer of the team. We marched in President Lyndon B. Johnson's inaugural parade in 1965. We were bussed to Washington, D.C.

and put up in an old army barracks, then bussed back to Kings Point the following day. What an adventure.

Later that year, I began dating a girl named Sue. A nice young lady from Mexico. Her Mother had married a rich Mexican doctor and they all lived in Mexico City. She had come to America to attend Secretarial School. We dated and she and I went to many Academy functions for the rest of my second class year and into my First Class year. You could say, we were "going steady". Sue and I also attended the Academy Ring Dance (where I got my Academy ring). Over Christmas leave in 1965, we became engaged. Susan flew back home to Mexico.

Graduation loomed and with it came the Coast Guard license exam. It lasted six grueling days, covering seamanship, navigation, and Rules of the Road, which include maritime law. I failed seamanship on my first attempt, but passed on the second after a weekend of intense study. In June, my parents drove to New York for the ceremony. I received my diploma, a Coast Guard License and a Commission as an Ensign in the Naval Reserve. I also received $8,000 from my parents, since the Merchant Marine Academy is Federally funded, my tuition was free. They rewarded me with the College fund they had set aside for me. God, and Mom and Dad had really come through for me.

During my first class year, each Cadet was expected to intern at a Shipping Company to learn how the shipping industry operates. With help from my Uncle, a long time respected Humble employee, I had secured an internship with the Marine Division of Humble Oil in Houston, Texas. All the ships were still "Esso" ships, the name was not changed to Exxon until the 70's.

By June 1, I had my first assignment as a Third Mate aboard the SS Esso Florence, moored in Bucksport, Maine. The boy from Tuscaloosa, who once broke his arm trying to fly now held a license to cross oceans. My parents once again came through for me and drove me to my first ship as a Third Mate, to begin the next chapter of my life in Bucksport, Maine.

CHAPTER 4:

EARLY CAREER: JOURNEY AS MERCHANT MARINE WATCH OFFICER

My first job serving as a ship officer, was on the SS Esso Florence. I already knew how exciting and terrifying working on the ocean could be. When I finished at the Academy I was totally confident and thrilled about my career. At the age of 21, I had the responsibility of a 19,000 ton ship hauling thousands of barrels of heating oil and 45 men as well as myself.

I remembered the moment when the Captain assigned me the midnight shift, known as the "EIGHT TO TWELVE". The Captain didn't ask me if I was ready – he simply gave me the order to do my job. It was a new opportunity for me, and it was overwhelming to say the least. I was so relieved at midnight when the second officer arrived at the bridge, and relieved me from the bridge. I walked off the bridge directly to my cabin. I had been completely alone for four hours. What a feeling.

As I stood watch on the bridge it was quiet except for the hum of the ship's systems. Navigation instruments beeped rhythmically, and the ship creaked slightly as it moved through the water. Outside, the ocean was vast and dark, except for a few lights ashore and other vessels at sea, stretching endlessly. Above me, the stars shined clearly, but they seemed impossibly distant. I held tightly to my training, but my heart was pounding.

There's something about massive responsibility when you must work with it. In theory, the job was simple: avoid collisions and stay on course. The autopilot handled the steering; but mentally I had to remain alert, checking the radar, monitoring our position, and keep in communication with my senior officer, as needed. I had help from two able bodied seamen and one ordinary seaman. One manned the bow, one the stern, and one stayed on the bridge with me and steered the ship, when not on autopilot. They served as lookouts and would report anything unusual that might happen.

Despite the pressure, I relied on my training and my instincts, praying all the time. I followed procedures, which I repeatedly had drilled into me while I was at the Academy. I made it through that first watch. When the clock struck midnight, I felt comfortable and took a long breath after working four hours – I felt as though I had "passed" I finally felt like a real sea officer.

Later, I learned something that surprised me. The Captain had been just one deck below, keeping the same watch in case something happened. He never had to step in. I never new until we docked that he had been there. I thanked him profusely for trusting me so much. God was good to me. I made it through that first four hours without incident!

His quiet presence showed me what leadership really means. He didn't interfere, but he never abandoned me either. That silent support gave me more confidence than any lesson ever could.

Of course, not everything at sea was as smooth as my first night on the ship. One incident in Baton Rouge, Louisiana, stands out in my memory. We were docking to unload heating oil. This was a routine matter. Starboard (right side) to shore, a tug boat was tied to the ship at the front.

The process was supposed to be foolproof: dock, shut the valve at the pier head, unbolt the metal plate covering the pipe, open the valve to the ship's tank, open the valve at the refinery tank, begin the transfer of oil. But someone ashore forgot to close the dock's valve before the tank was opened on the ship. As soon as the plate was struck, the oil exploded out like a cannon shot. A powerful stream of heating oil, nearly eight inches in diameter, shot out with terrifying force. It was flammable fuel. Crew members were instantly shocked. There was no time to think about anything other than get out of the way.

I was on the bridge, unable to do much except shout and hope someone would shut the valve. Fortunately, the emergency shut off system at the refinery acted rapidly and shut the necessary valve, averting panic at that situation. The system was shut down before it escalated. We got away from the dock to prevent further spillage into the Mississippi River.

By sheer luck and careful maneuvering, we avoided a disaster and eventually tied up safely. No one was injured, and the crew cleaned up the ship with the passage of time. But it could have ended in disaster if the situation had not been handled quickly. One spark could have caused an explosion that would have destroyed our ship and part of the refinery.

Another time, we were loading xylene in Baytown, Texas. Xylene is a highly flammable chemical used in jet fuel to make it burn. We had over 30,000 barrels on board and were almost finished when a large ship came speeding up the channel where our ship was undocking. We blew our emergency alarms, radio waring, and reversed engines of our ship immediately. The tugboat at our bow pushed in reverse as hard as it could. It was pure madness. The incoming ship **never** stopped, it just kept on going. It scraped along our bow. Fortunately, its sharp bow didn't hit us.

If there had been a spark, the xylene would have exploded the ship, exploded most of the town of Baytown, Texas along with thousands of people, and the nearby refinery as well. Once again. the grace of God saved us all. A maritime surveyor inspected our ship the next day and there were no leaks. We were able to sail, but on one ever forgot that night!

These sort of experiences made me trust in something greater than myself. I began to understand that even with planning for contingency situations, some things were just out of my control. Sometimes measures cannot be taken with immediate effect.

On those long, quiet nights with the sounds of the sea, I often prayed. The sea gives you a lot of time to think. Some men get frustrated or annoyed by the loneliness. As for me, those hours of loneliness became a moment of survival and to think deeply about myself and my future.

Life at sea is a strange thing. You're surrounded by people, yet you can feel incredibly alone. Most of the crew, about twenty-seven men, sharing the ship. There were no women. Everyone had a role: The Captain, chief mate, second and third mates, engineers, cooks, and seamen. The work was nonstop in port. At sea, time slowed down, but the weight of responsibility never disappeared.

When I was off duty, I thought a lot about my home. I missed my family my friends, even the little things like going to the store, watching a movie and having dinner with my family. Those everyday moments became my precious memories during those tough and challenging years at sea.

With Exxon, the typical schedule was three months on the ship, followed by a month and a half off, with pay. But that schedule was subject to change if the sea office's managing staff asked you to stay on the ship. Sometimes you might only be home for a few weeks before they might call you back. That unpredictability was quite tough for everyone, particularly our families.

At this time, I was married to my first wife, Sue. We met during my second class year and continued dating through the first part of my senior (first class) year at Kings Point. She was visiting campus with some of her friends and sat next to me while watching a football game. I performed with the Drill Team at half time, after which we started talking with each other. She had a positive attitude with an optimistic smile that I adored until my first try at married life ended.

Sue was studying to be a secretary and lived on Long Island with a friend, her friend's mother and younger brother. They shared a small house in Levittown. Every night, they climbed up a set of stairs and tucked themselves in the attic. She never complained about having to sleep in the attic.

We dated for many months, and around Christmas of my senior year, she took a flight to Birmingham to meet my family. We toured the town, visited places that I haunted during my childhood, and by the end of the trip, I proposed to her. Her answer was *"Yes!"*

But our marriage didn't last. The long distance between us took an emotional toll that didn't help her. While I was at sea, Sue began having an affair. I found out about my wife's affair through one of my family members. One night, during my midnight watch at Bayonne, New Jersey, a registered letter arrived from Sue's lawyer. I opened the package with dread -

and my heart's feelings went up and down. These were divorce papers. Once I opened the letter I was stunned. I thought about leaving the ship immediately, but a wise second mate pulled me aside and advised: *"Don't do what she expects – finish your job and stay on the ship. Go home when you get officially off the ship."* I followed his advice. When I finally returned to Baytown, Texas, my life changed drastically. I left the ship, went to my rental flat and found it empty. I went to call on my Aunt and Uncle. I told them about Sue and they told me that Sue had been misbehaving while I was at sea. I went to her lawyer's office and he and I divided our common property. I called Sue because she had all my clothes. I had a pain that remained deep in my heart for a long time. No one gets married thinking it will end after only 18 months. My parents saw her in California many years later. My Dad didn't even recognize her (she had put on a bit of weight). Sue recognized my Mother, however, and they spoke and that was the last time she was ever mentioned again.

Having given the car to Sue, I had a friend drive me to the Chevrolet dealership in Baytown. There I bought the last 1968 silver Corvette convertible in town. My friend and his girlfriend and several of her friends went riding around Baytown in my new Corvette. It was great fun. The Corvette was a "chick magnet". But, about 4 weeks later I discovered **no** insurance company would insure me with a Corvette. I had wrecked my Oldsmobile 442 just a few months before, and, I was now divorced. Back to the dealership to trade my dream car for a six cylinder Oldsmobile cutlass (something the insurance company was willing to cover). Shortly after this, my Mother asked me why I just didn't call her – she told me she would have been glad to put the car in her name and to use her car insurance. Life's little ups and downs. But, what a four weeks it was!

Life at sea is incredibly hard, particularly on relationships. Nearly every married man I sailed with had a similar story. The constant absences, missed holidays, and unexpected redeployments wore people down.

Still, I learned a lot in those early years. The experience shaped me. It made me stronger. My faith became an anchor. I learned that leadership doesn't mean knowing everything. It means staying steady when you don't know it all. I discovered that even in your loneliest moments, you are not truly alone. God is always there for you.

Those first voyages helped form the man I have become. They taught me to believe in myself, to stay humble, and to keep going even when life throws hard challenges at you. .

CHAPTER 5:

LOVE AND FAMILY

Some of life's biggest changes begin in the most unexpected places. For me, it was a cold winter day at Penn Station. Christmas had just passed, and I was returning to the last part of my senior year at the Merchant Marine Academy after being at home for the holidays. It was the first day of the subway strike in New York on the 3rd of January 1966, and Penn Station was maddingly **over-crowded** with people trying to make their way back out to Long Island by one of the few means still available. There were long lines, frustrated travelers, and a general air of confusion. I was in uniform, tired from traveling all night and dragging my heavy suitcase by a belt, this was before suitcases had wheels, and found myself behind a woman with an armful of magazines.

She caught my eye right away, a petite blonde, and carrying several magazines: Time, Life, and Sports Illustrated. I couldn't resist saying, *"Wow, you must read a lot!"*. With a quick, amused smile, she replied, *"Well I work for* **Time/Life** *so I get them every Monday"*.

That sparked a conversation between us, one of the easiest and most natural. Her name was Janie. She was clever, funny, and calm in all the chaos. When she said she was headed to Little Neck, I told her that I was headed to Great Neck, just one stop past hers. She knew about the Academy. We rode the train together, talking like old friends. At the station in Little Neck, just as she stepped on to the platform, I asked for her phone number. She called it out to me, and I quickly wrote it down, as fortunately, I had a piece of paper and pen with me. (She later told me she never expected me to call….but I did.)

When I called a few days later, she remembered me instantly. I invited her to a basketball game at the Academy. *"Sure, I'll come"* she said, and, because I offered to pick her up by Taxi, she said *"Don't be silly, I've got my own car"*. She came in her cherry-red 1965 Pontiac convertible. She had style and confidence, and I liked that. We went to the game, had a great time, and that was our first official date.

Two weeks later, I invited her to the "First Class" ski trip to the Concord Hotel in upstate New York. She agreed without hesitation. Janie met me at the Academy, and we drove to the Ski Lodge together, meeting with the rest of the cadets and their dates. When we got to the hotel, I realized I'd made a mistake as I had booked only one room with two beds. Janie looked me square in the eye and said *"I'm not sleeping with you. I'm NOT sharing a room with you."* Fair enough. I respected that.

I scrambled for a solution. By chance, a maid walked out of a freshly cleaned room. I acted like it was mine, tipped her a few bucks, and stayed there alone. The next morning, I stuffed chewing gum in the door lock and hung a "Do Not Disturb" sign to avoid questions.

Janie and I spent the weekend sledding, throwing snowballs, and riding in a horse-drawn sleigh. It was magical, simple, fun, and honest. I felt something real with her. Nothing about her reminded me of Sue.

Speaking of that first marriage, it started going downhill almost immediately. On the second night of our honeymoon, my ex-wife told me she'd decided, after talking to a friend, that we would only be intimate every other week. That set the tone.

The rest of the honeymoon was tense and cold. I knew I'd made a mistake.

Janie and I dated steadily for two months after our Ski weekend, until Janie became a stewardess for American Airlines and moved to Dallas, Texas, in April, 1966. However, one time, when my ship came into Newark, New Jersey's Esso Refinery, after we docked I had the evening free, so I called American Airlines and learned that Janie was due in at 5:30 pm at the Newark Airport. Off I went, I made it to the jetway in time to see the passengers departing. When the crew started to leave, I asked if Janie was with them and they said *"Yes, and she's still on board."* (Things were very different in 1966). I ran on board, and there she was with her back to me picking up the cabin. When I tapped her shoulder she turned around and the look of total surprise and joy appeared on her face. I returned to the ship on time knowing I had found my true love.

I made a huge mistake by rushing into marriage with Sue. I was young, adrift, and not thinking clearly. It didn't last long. When I returned from sea one day, I found the new bank account I had opened after my divorce, and had my payroll going into, was empty! None of my bills had been paid and I was broke! The bank had mistakenly deposited my earnings into the wrong account that I had no access to. Thankfully, the bank admitted the error and reimbursed me. Sue didn't take any money dishonestly, but the marriage was built on sand.

What I didn't know at the time was that Sue came from a very wealthy family. Her grandfather owned Grumman Aircraft, a major name in aviation. Her mother had been a New York debutante who married a wealthy Mexican doctor. Sue held dual citizenship. I had no clue about any of this before we married, and honestly, it wouldn't have made a difference.

After my divorce, I thought of Janie all the time. One day, I docked in New York, I called the number she had given me two years earlier. Her mother answered. She was polite, but made it clear I wasn't welcome because they thought I had abandoned her, which was understandable. She said Janie wasn't there and would not give me her number. Turns out Janie had also gone through a rough marriage. Her husband had been very abusive, however, when she flew home to New York for vacation after her divorce she happened to casually ask *"Has anyone heard from Bob Dunham?"* There was a dead silence for a few minutes, but then her younger sister looked at her with a grin, even though her mother had replied *"No"*.

Soon, a letter showed up at my parent's home and it was from Janie. We started writing to each other again, and it didn't take long for old feelings to come back. While at sea we stayed in touch by letter and phone calls, when I was in port (no cell phones in the 1960's). She had stopped flying and was a secretary in Denton, Texas. There were nightly poker games on board ship and I sent all my winnings to Denton. I came to Denton, Texas, where she was living, for a visit.

After completing my three years of obligatory Sea Duty for my degree, license, and commission in the Naval Reserve, I was tired of sailing on tankers. I decided to quit Exxon and join the Masters, Mates and Pilots Union. The Captain came on the bridge while I was working, ranting about my clothes being in the dryer. *"You live like a Pig!"* How could he dry his clothes with mine in the dryer. He assumed the watch and ordered me to move my clothes. Of course, I did so immediately, returned to the bridge and told him to find a replacement for me – I quit. He went back to bed in a huff. The next morning I packed and was gone before noon. Fortunately, we were in Baytown where I had my apartment and my car. The first thing I did was call Janie in Denton, Texas. I repacked and headed for Denton. About a week later, my father called Janie's number….The Houston Headquarters of Esso Oil Company, Marine Division, had called my father's home in Birmingham looking for me. The house cleaner happened to be working that day and answered the phone. She took a phone number and called my Dad who then called me. When I answered Janie's phone my Dad said *"I was hoping I'd find you at this number."* He passed on Esso's number, I called immediately. Esso offered me a shore job as a Ship's Agent in Paulsboro, New Jersey.

I accepted the job with Esso in their shore office at Paulsboro, New Jersey. I called Janie at work and said *"Why don't you come with me? I have to be there in a week."* Her reply was sharp but clear *"Not unless you marry me."* I didn't hesitate, I bought a ring – I asked her to marry me that night. I packed up all my belongings (few as they were) loaded the car and headed to Paulsboro, New Jersey. I was number 3 in a three-man office. Our job was to meet and greet all ships associated with Esso scheduled to load or discharge in Paulsboro, the Esso port for Philadelphia, Pennsylvania. The port was on the east side of the Schuylkill River, Philadelphia was on the west. The office had a tugboat assigned to it which we had to schedule to meet each ship to assist with docking and undocking. The tug also took barges of heating oil or gasoline across the river and back.

Janie drove in her little red Volkswagen to Jackson Mississippi where she met my parents. They drove to Birmingham together, and then my Mother and Janie drove to New Jersey together where we "tied the knot" in a beautiful church in Woodbury, New Jersey. We got married and we began our new life together. Our honeymoon was a road trip to Virginia Beach, Williamsburg, Virginia, and Washington, D.C. Afterward, Janie and I settled into our new life, bought a tiny lakefront house in Almonesson, New Jersey that had a small swimming lake out front. A two bedroom, 2 bath home with living room, kitchen, and ¾ basement - cost (1969 price) $14,000. It was our first home. We also adopted a miniature schnauzer, Rex.

A year later, Janie became pregnant with our daughter, Tracy. I remember pacing the hospital waiting room waiting for news. When she finally gave birth to our daughter, the joy was amazing. Janie had a very rough delivery, compounded by the fact that her doctor went home for dinner just as they administered Petrossian to help expedite labor - Tracy had managed to turn herself completely during this time. Janie suffered several hours unnecessarily. When the doctor finally returned, he immediately discovered the problem – he turned Tracy and they immediately went to the delivery room where Tracy was born. When I confronted the doctor, I realized there wasn't much I could do.

When we brought Tracy home, our little schnauzer, Rex, who had been the center of our attention, met her with confusion. Later when we allowed him to actually "check her out", he tried to pee on her! I reacted quickly and put him outside. That was the end of that behavior. It took time for Rex to adjust, but he became a very loyal friend to the baby.

Due to changing priorities, Janie and I decided to move the family to Birmingham, Alabama in 1972. Our home sold for $24,000, a nice profit for a three year investment (although we did make some necessary improvements.) The job I was counting on in Alabama proved to be less than it was made to be and Janie went back to work.

Our son Christoper was born in 1976. Life became a rhythm: work, parenting, and moving. One night Tracy spiked a 105-degree fever and convulsed. Janie panicked and gave her to me. I told her to run a tepid bath in the tub. I held Tracy's head above the water while we waited for the ambulance. A neighbor, who turned out to be someone I knew from high school, drove me to the hospital even though she had a fresh cast on her arm. Janie had ridden with Tracy in the ambulance. A cop pulled us over for speeding, but after I explained the situation, he let us go. Thankfully, Tracy recovered, but continued to experience petite-mal syndrome until she was 5. But that night still lingers in my mind.

After the incident with Tracy, we decided to look for a home. We found a nice new suburban neighborhood in Pelham, Alabama, a bedroom community of Birmingham. The house cost less than $50,000, was 3 bedroom, 2 bath with ½ acre yard and ½ basement. Hom prices were on the rise. We were enjoying ourselves, planting trees and flowers. A Magnolia tree we planted all those years ago is still there – grown huge, dominating the yard.

Janie and I tried to teach our children to love and obey the LORD and always follow the Golden Rule. They still remember the lessons, but like all people, they forget until some crisis comes along.

We're proud of both our children, as they have become the best versions of them selves. Tracy became a nurse and earned her doctorate in Neonatal care. Christoper became an Eagle Scout and pursued his career path at the Merchant Marine Academy with confidence. We sent them both to Christian schools, believing it would give them strong values. In her senior year, Tracy transferred to a public school for her senior year, and graduated with honors, saying she had already learned most of the curriculum at the Christian school!

Tracy married Joe, a music engineer and ultimately a Professor at Belmont College in Nashville, Tennessee. But the big wedding never happened. A clash between Tracy and Janie over the color or the dress she planned to wear to the wedding led the couple to elope to Colorado.

After some time, we became grandparents. Our first granddaughter Clare, became a lawyer at age 25, what an amazing achievement. We watched her walk the stage at graduation just filled with pride. Her brother, Owen, graduated pre-med from the University of Tennessee just two weeks later. Then, our Son's daughter, Amelia, graduated from Vidalia High School in Vidalia, Georgia and has been accepted at Georgia Southern for the fall semester. Our youngest granddaughter, Eleanor, will finish high school next year. Every milestone feels like a gift from God. Our 10 year old grandson also had honors at his school for maintaining an "A" average for his entire 3rd grade class year!

Love didn't come easily in my life. But when it arrived in the form of a woman with an armload of magazines and a red convertible I knew it was worth holding on to. Janie and I built a life that was real, sometimes messy, often difficult, but always filled with deep affection, love, and loyalty. We have raised our children, built a home, and carried each other through the storms of life.

It all started in a very crowded train station, with just a simple hello. Here we are living our lives happily with each other, after some 56 years! I can proudly say Janie filled an emptiness in my life and poured in a lot of happiness, success, and love. I cherish every moment with her at every step of our lives. Praise the Lord for Love!

CHAPTER 6:

CAREER TRANSITIONS AND

ACHIEVEMENTS

I had been out at sea as watch officer. I spent three years sailing on Esso tankers learning how to manage a crew. This helped me organize and correct problems in the Parts Department. Sailing teaches you discipline. The discipline sticks to your bones. You learn to respect hierarchy, keep your word, and anticipate problems before they become disaster. Above all, you learn to respect the people you work with. When you are on a ship hundreds of miles from shore your life depends on them.

Life aboard a tanker isn't a small thing. There's a certain rhythm to watch cycles, crew changes, engine hums, and the ever-present feel of steel and sea air. I lived in those cycles. I learned what it meant to stand a bridge watch at 2:00 am in the pitch black, scanning a radar screen, and trusting your guts as much as your training.

When I returned to land and took the job as a ship's agent in Paulsboro, New Jersey, that time at sea suddenly became my greatest advantage. Other colleagues came fresh out of college with polished shoes and business degrees. They knew how to file paperwork, but they didn't speak "the language" we spoke on ships, but I did.

I knew the hierarchy on board, the expectations of Captains, the gruff language of engineers, and the quiet needs of exhausted crewmen after a long haul. Because I knew what they needed, often before they had any issues.

One day, I was chosen for a special task: delivering $8,000 in cash to the SS Manhattan, a converted supertanker-turned-icebreaker, docked in Philadelphia, before its historic

Northwest Passage voyage. It wasn't only a delivery – it was a test of trust.

We didn't take any risks. I had a directive from the Philadelphia Police Department who accompanied me as an escort. We drove across the Walt Whitman Bridge into a part of the city that had seen better days. The ship loomed over the docks like a giant steel cathedral and its walkway stretching what seemed like fifty feet into the sky.

I gripped the briefcase tightly as we climbed. Once aboard, the Captain gave me a respectful nod, he recognized a fellow seaman when he saw one. We walked into the ship's office, exchanged pleasantries, and I handed over the cash. He signed the receipt with a positive gesture. Then, in true maritime fashion, we sat down together for lunch. No fuss, no formality, just good food and professional respect toward each other.

I didn't get to sail on the Manhattan. I even told the people I'd wash dishes if they needed me to. But they needed someone with more icebreaking experience and less tanker background. Still, I had my moment on that historic vessel, and that was enough for me.

Ultimately, we left Paulsboro and moved to Birmingham. I joined the family business: *Dunham GMC Truck Company*. My uncle brought me in to handle warranties for clients. I thought it would be a simple job, but it wasn't. Within weeks, I discovered a scam that had cost our business thousands of dollars. Every time a customer bought a new transmission or rear axle, we charged a $300 core fee, which was refundable, if they returned the used part. It was simple enough, however, one long-time employee had his own system. He'd take the core, sell it himself on the black market, and pocket $300. Customers would come back expecting a refund, and we'd be out this money. This had been going on for years. I took responsibility for taking this information to the Accounts Department. I had saved $1,500 the first week, probably more when I took this information to my uncle, he gave me the go-ahead to fire the man. That was one of the hardest conversations I've ever had. He cried, and he begged. He said he had a family, but I wasn't about to let someone steal from the company.

That was the beginning.

A few months later, a factory representative visited our dealership. He spent two weeks observing every department. When he finished, he told my Uncle and Father something I'll never forget:

Bob is the only one here I'd trust to run the Parts Department."

I still remember the moment I became the manager of the Parts Department of *Dunham GMC Truck Company*. It wasn't a celebration. There was no champagne or high-fives. It was just a quiet nod from my father, who had received a phone call from my uncle, informing him of the promotion and asking him to let me know, because he was out of town. To me it was one of the most significant transitions of my life. A turning point. My life began shifting from oil-stained uniforms to shop floors and spread sheets, and computer read-outs. I had $120,000 in inventory and six employees, three of whom were making more than I was. The previous manager was promoted sideways to an outside sales role and kept his salary. Another was a senior man with 20 years service. Yet I was the "boss" and responsible for any discrepancies I found in the Parts Department of our company.

I didn't complain. Instead I made a deal with my uncle: *"If we sell $100,000 in a month, each of us in the Parts Department gets $150 bonus money."* He laughed in my face saying: *"You'll never do it."*

That first month we hit $102,000. The next month, we had sales of $120,000. The following month we sold $135,000. My team was motivated. We all got this $150/month bonus until I left the company. I had organized every employee in a professional manner. The Parts Department was finally running like a well-oiled machine.

When the inventory time came, my uncle warned me: *"We're always $10,000 to $15,000 short."* I thought – **"Not this time"**.

We did a full count of inventory, every washer and every bolt. When we finished, our inventory was less than $2.00 short. My Uncle raised an eyebrow. He was expecting a shortage of $15,000 or more. *"Well,"* he grunted, *"should've been doing this all the time."*

We received no bonus, no thank you. Just another day. But I didn't do it for the praise, I did it because it was for the betterment of the company that had my name on the roof! Six months later, we did it again with an even larger inventory with still no shortage.

Then came a call from Peterbilt Motors, they offered me a job as a Regional Parts Rep, working out of their Peterbilt Plant in Nashville, Tennessee. I was offered $1,450/month that was almost double what I was making. I accepted the job at Peterbilt. That job took me across the Midwest from Chicago to Minneapolis, from Green Bay to Indianapolis. I visited dealerships, advised Parts Managers, and helped streamline operations as well. I was good at all of it.

Eventually, I got promoted again to the east coast region: Boston, New York, and the rest of the Atlantic corridor were part of my responsibility. But the job came with a cost. The company changed its travel policy. I would be required to be on the road three weeks a month. My wife was tired of being a single parent and gave me a ultimatum that I'll never forget. *"I married a sailor once, I don't want to do that again."*

So I made the choice. I resigned to stay home. Once away from Peterbilt, I wore many hats. An exterminator and then Sales Manager, then promoted to Branch Manager for Orkin Exterminating.

While living in Charlotte, North Carolina, I got my Real Estate License, and have been working in Real Estate, both in Charlotte and after our move to the mountains, here in Franklin, North Carolina. Each role brought the same principles: discipline, integrity, and a solution to every problem.

Looking back, I realized that the transition from deck to desk wasn't about giving up the sea, it was about carrying the sea with me, it's lessons, its order and I respect every job I did.

What did I learn? Leadership isn't about titles or salaries. It's about doing hard things when no one helps you out or you are alone at the job. It's about rooting out corruptions, even when it's difficult to trace. It's about walking into chaos and creating order and doing new things that support both me and the company I work for.

I have never stopped being a sailor regardless of what job I held. I have followed the same principles my Mother taught me:

1. Be Honest
2. Don't Lie
3. Treat everyone with respect, exactly as you would want to be treated.
4. Above all, follow God's directions.

CHAPTER 7:

FAITH AND PERSONAL GROWTH

For my personal growth: I was not yet old enough to actual test my faith in God. Somewhere in that murky space between youthful energy and adult responsibility. I faced one of the most confusing and painful lessons of my life. A time when everything I thought, and I understood about career, trust , personal growth, and friendship revealed in front of me to be false.

It started with a promotion that should have been a gift for me. I had been working with Exxon, handling responsibilities as a ship's agent in Paulsboro, New Jersey. Everything seemed to be going smoothly. The Captains trusted me. My team was well-managed and I took the responsibility for any task given to me. I knew the ships, spoke their language, understood what they needed before they asked. My Maritime license game me credibility, and my years at sea gave me instinct. I considered my boss, at the time to be a friend. He assisted with my marriage to Janie and we got along well. I was not aware I had done anything wrong, but one day I received a formal document which was an end-of-assignment report filled with disparaging remarks and I hardly recognized myself in it. The man who wrote it had never spoken to me about any issues. He had never pulled me aside or even hinted that I was failing in any part of my job. Yet, in a few cold paragraphs, he dismantled my reputation.

I remember sitting in my small home reading it line by line. My hands trembled. My wife and I had so many dreams build on the foundation of this job. *"What do we do now?"* she gently asked. I just didn't have an answer. But I remember saying this: *"God must have a plan. I just can't see it yet."*

That night I prayed more honestly than I had in a long time. Not with fancy words, just confusion and desperation: *"LORD, You gave me this job. Why would You let it fall apart like this?"*

I received no immediate answer and it was silent. But there was something else taking place under God's plan. Not a loud, dramatic peace, just a still, small voice, like a whisper: *"Be Patient, I've got this."*

Shortly after this a new boss took over – after working under him for six months, he couldn't see any of the problems outlined in that awful fitness report from the previous boss. Additionally, I worked at the Esso Ship's Office in Baltimore, Maryland (which was the hub for the eastern seaboard for Esso), the "big boss" found absolutely no issue with me either. The new boss' fitness report helped allay some of the fears I had about performing well.

During this time I truly began to lean on my faith. Not just in Church on Sundays, but in real life. In the hard, ugly spaces where things didn't make sense. Ultimately, we left New Jersey and moved to Birmingham. I didn't know what was coming, but I knew I was done pretending that every closed door was a failure. Sometimes, a door shuts because you're not meant to stay where you are. Sometimes, it's the only way God can push you toward something greater.

Over the years, I've had plenty of reasons to doubt people. One of the biggest lessons I've learned, particularly in business, is that not everyone who smiles at you means you are doing well.

There was a man I went into business with after my departure from Peterbilt, in Nashville. He was a church friend, which is sometimes how these stories start. He invited me and another mutual church friend to go into the heating/air conditioning business. He said, we'd be partners. He also stated that everything was set up for this business. His wife would handle the paperwork and books. We'd help build a brand. It sounded like a good plan – it wasn't.

His wife, who handled the books, and was funneling money out of our company into a new venture of her own – a health food business – featuring Shaklee products – vitamins and supplements of all kinds.

While people trusted us for installations and service, the bills began to pile up – we were having trouble making payroll, even though money was coming into the company. When the collapse came, he tried to pin the debts on me and our partner. Legally, he had grounds. Ethically, that's a different story. I trusted him. I even prayed with him about the business and other issues he had with his family. It took everything I had to walk away and not let the bitterness take root in me. I forgave him – not because he deserved it, but because I did.

Forgiveness, I've learned, isn't about excusing bad behavior. It's about freeing yourself from it. Carrying anger is like drinking poison and expecting someone else to die. So, I forgave, even though he never apologized and when we saw him at church, he refused to speak and kept his distance eventually leaving the church and going elsewhere.

Looking back, I can see the God's plan more clearly. God used those disappointments and failures to teach me how to depend on Him, not on titles, bosses, contracts, or other people.

I had recently started my own business (a termite/pest control business called DoRite Pest Control), in Nashville, Tennessee. When my mother passed away, I was able to go to Birmingham and leave the business in good hands with my partner. If I had remained at the other job, I would have missed that final week with her. When my father was completely bereft, after Mother died, I was able to be there and offer support as a son. Sometimes, we only understand God's mercy by looking backwards!

Politics were always a part of our family fiber. My father was a staunch Republican. He had served under Eisenhower in World War II, and he carried that loyalty to his grave. We weren't a political family in the modern sense. We didn't yell at the television or argue over dinner. We believed in responsibility, in limited government, in working hard, and earning what kept your family running.

Those values shaped how I led teams, how I treated employees, and how I dealt with problems on jobs. Don't expect handouts, don't complain, and don't make excuses. Just get up and do your job.

During my time in the Navy and traveling overseas, I saw things that made me appreciate America even more. What a great country to grow up in!

In Taiwan, children would line up on the docks as our ships came in. Each morning, we received five bars of soap in our officer's quarters. Why? Union rules. We didn't need them all, of course. None of us could use five bars of soap in a day. But the kids down below could. So, we'd toss the extra bars of soap – like small flying treasures – into the crows of children. At the time, we thought it was funny. Later, I realized it was heartbreaking. They needed that soap. It was their treasure and we threw it away like it was nothing.

Those trips showed me how uneven the world is. Not everyone is born with the same opportunities. Not everyone gets a second chance. So, when you are blessed enough to have health, education, and freedom, which you owe to the U.S. Military men and women, you owe the world – do something worthwhile to help others in need.

One of the most painful moments came because I trusted a young woman who worked with me. She was optimistic, hard working, and going through a difficult married life. She had five children and needed the job I gave her. Her husband was extremely abusive, addicted to drugs and threatened her. I helped her and tried to give her a new start. But pain does strange things to people. One day, I got a call and learned that this woman had been involved in a crime with her husband and sister! Her husband forced her to drive the "get-away" car in a drug-related robbery. She swore she had no choice – she said he had threatened her and her children – even though she was pregnant with their sixth child at the time. Maybe it was true – maybe it wasn't. People at our church had warned us that they were not to be trusted – but we trusted in the woman. It turns out they were right. My wife and I trusted her but she betrayed that trust and lied to us on many occasions to get and keep our trust. I still don't regret helping her. I got a better more clear view of the grace of God in my life.

Faith isn't just for pews and Sunday morning. It's for real life. It's for broken deals, the bad bosses, the betrayals, and the doubts. Faith is what helped me up when everything fell apart. Even now, I can look back at every setback and say with certainty: Giod was there every time. He promises never to leave us or forsake us. God was with me even in the storms of life.

CHAPTER 8:

HOBBIES, TRAVEL AND OTHER
INTERESTS

Some people collect trophies or medals. I have the hobby of collecting stamps. Each one, small and silent, tell a story of time and place, of forgotten places and shifting borders. My collection didn't start out as anything grand, and it was just a boyhood fascination with the colorful squares that arrived in envelopes from far-off lands. But, over time it grew into something much more: a map of history, a mirror of patience and a bridge between generations. My father gave me his collection when I was nine. He had started when he was 8 or 9. Some of the stamps he gave me are worth hundreds or thousands of dollars now. A legacy for me to pass along to my son.

The pride of my collection is the 1893 Columbian Exposition Fair stamp. They celebrated the 400th anniversary of Columbus' voyage and included seventeen beautifully detailed stamps. My favorite is the crown jewel, which is the $5.00 stamp. It isn't the design, though that alone could draw the eye of any serious philatelist. My son found it in an auction catalog, it was "used", but an authentic stamp. He bid on it, won it, and then surprised me. He said: *"If you pay half, you can have it."* We split the cost, $400/each. But in truth, the stamp because priceless to me. It was more than paper and ink. It was a gift from a son who understood what it mean to his father. That makes it priceless!

Stamp collecting taught me more than history. It taught me attention to detail. It taught me patience, the kind of patience you need when you're dealing with people, with machinery, with business partners who don't keep their word. Stamp don't ditch you. They don't cheat you. But they reward discipline. Over the years, they became a quiet companion to my chaotic professional life. In some ways, the discipline required in stamp collecting mirrored the order I found in the Navy. When you're cataloging thousands of stamps, labeling them, learning their backstories, you find yourself immersed in a quieter world. It gave my mind a kind of rest. I couldn't always find in my professional life. There's something calming about carefully flipping through stamp albums, tongs in hand, positioning each square precisely into its mount. It's like conducting a symphony in silence.

Another companion to my stamp collection is chess. I learned to play chess when I was eight. A neighbor child taught me how each piece moved, and I was hooked. I didn't become a grandmaster, but I became something better, a lifelong chess player. Chess is a mirror. It showed me how to approach challenges with care and strategic tools to apply through common sense. Always thinking three move ahead, but no afraid to take a bold step if the moment demands it.

In college, I met my match literally. My best friend and I would play with each other nearly every day. For three years, we played chess and nothing else. He'd win one and I'd win the next. It became a rhythm and part of our friendship. We'd sit quietly across from each other, the board between us, moving pawns like dancers on a stage. The game taught me grace in defeat and humility in victory. Decades later, we still send each other Christmas cards. We reminisce, not about grades or classes, but about the games. At that time, he pulled off a rook sacrifice that I never saw coming or the match I won in six moves using a trap I had spent months in getting to perfection.

Travel added brighter color to the quieter pastimes of my life. My favorite place was Hawaii. Not just because of the beauty of the palm trees and ocean sunsets, but because I went there with my wife twice. The first time was from Dunham GMC. We'd hit our parts sales targets and then as a reward, the company flew Janie and I, and the Service Manager and his wife out to Hawaii for a week of fun, touring and relaxations. Everything was paid for by Peterbilt Motors. We stayed in a resort that was beautiful, and it barely seemed real. Th second time, we saved some money and Janie and I went by ourselves. There is something about being in Hawaii that feels like paradise, particularly with someone you love. We tried to imagine living there, but we knew it was just a dream. Still, it was enough to have walked the beaches hand in hand hearing the waves whisper along the shore.

I also visited Hawaii under very different circumstances with the Navy. I requested training there, and when I arrived with a group of officers, we discovered the exercise was cancelled. But the Navy had already booked rooms for us. Mine was off-base so they gave me a rental car and a hotel suite. I spent two weeks driving around Oahu, attending a few token meetings, and enjoying the island and its gorgeous scenery. Sometimes, life just gives you a phenomenal break without asking.

In addition to collecting stamps and playing chess, I also enjoy painting with oils. Now, I'm not a professional artist. I don't sell my work in galleries or command big fees, but I do have a few paintings hanging in homes that aren't mine. One of them I gave to a former secretary of mine, a woman who had worked with me for years and became a kind of adopted daughter. She told me, she was offered $500 for it by a visitor. It was a painting of a Maine lighthouse. I'd saw a photo of it while visiting the Northeast with my daughter and granddaughter. She turned the offer down saying: *I couldn't ever sell it, Bob gave it to me."* You can't put a price on that.

My mother was a multi-talented woman, though a non-professional artist herself, she painted landscapes and still-life that carried the quiet dignity of someone painting not to impress, but to express. She encouraged me to continue my artwork. She purchased my first set of oil paints, and would sit with me for hours and taught me how to do sketching. Her praise meant the most to me, because she never handed it out freely. If she said something was good, it truly was.

Church has always been a big part of our life. Janie and I were active members of a Baptist congregation in Franklin, North Carolina. We went on missionary trips with another couple of friends from church to Massachusetts, Vermont and other parts of the Northeast, as well as the Outer Banks of

North Carolina. We helped run Vacation Bible School programs for small-town churches in Vermont, serving kids who didn't get a lot of attention. Those were some of the best years of our faith in God's service. Not all church experiences are good.

After our beloved Pastor retired, the church hired a younger man. Optimistic, passionate, devout and a blessing to all. But he struggled to support his family on a Pastor's salary, so he took a second job. That didn't sit well with the deacons. They forced him out, and half of the congregation left with him, including many of our friends. We stayed a little longer. The church hired another Pastor but he didn't preach the word of God. More people left. We did a Bible Study on Revelation with him and in the first session discovered just how bad things were (apparently he subscribed to the view that certain scriptures were interpreted incorrectly and he believed in a new interpretation) and we decided to leave ourselves and never went back.

Faith is something like art, stamps and chess, it must be built on trust in God and His ultimate plan. When the ground shifts too much, when people try to rewrite the truth for convenience, or for any reason, you must step away and don't involve yourself in that mistake.

We visited several other churches in our area before settling on one that preached the full gospel and all of the Bible and its truths. We found another church, just a bit smaller and quieter, but anchored in the same truth that has guided us since we were saved. We served where we could. Volunteered during holiday drive. We didn't need fancy buildings or booming choirs. We want sincerity, the true scripture of God, and a community of believers who believe in the veracity of God and his Holy Word.

These hobbies and quiet times with some loud moments all have shaped me. They've given me peace when the world was noisy. They've taught me discipline, patience, strategy, and the value of heritage. They've let me connect with others in ways that have nothing to do with money or power.

In the end, I think that's what life is about. The small and steady moments of joy. The fact that others overlook your faults and bring betterment to your life. The board games, and Bible verses are my lifeline. The several friendships had that have lasted a long time help me to be a better person, better friend, and I love and cherish them.

CHAPTER 9:

OVERCOMING ADVERSITY

Growing up, my dream car wasn't what you might typically expect from someone who admired muscle cars. Sure, the Pontiac GTO roared in my dreams, but I liked to do things differently. My eye was on the Oldsmobile 442! She was beautiful, unique, and stylish – red, of course, with a white top. I made myself a promise while attending Kings Point that after graduation, I would buy myself that car! It was more than a vehicle. It was a symbol of success, independence, and achieving something for myself.

Once I landed my job at Exxon and relocated to Baytown, Texas, I fulfilled my dream of owning this beauty. I went to Birmingham and bought that beautiful 442, loaded it with all my worldly possessions, and set out for Texas. The dealer had given me one piece of advice: don't push the car past 60 MPH, until you've gone at least 500 miles to break the engine in. So, despite my excitement and the urge to see what my new muscle car could do, I held steady at a modest 50-60 MPH. That wasn't easy Other drivers flew past me, flashing grins and mocking glances. I could hear their silent chuckles: *"Nice car, but slow ride."* But, when that speedometer hit 500 miles, I couldn't resist. A guy in a less impressive car tried to pass me doing about 65 – I floored it. The 442 leaped into action, and before I realized it, I was doing 80 and flying past him like he was standing still. It thrilled and terrified me. I slowed back down to 70. That was the moment I truly realized what kind of power I had in that car, and yet, that power proved to be a double-edged sword.

Life in Baytown settled in. I got married to Sue, and we used the car often. Then came the day that changed my whole outlook on safety. I had just returned from a ship, and a friend from the ship, along with his wife came over. The four of us hopped into the 441 and drove around. At a traffic light a stranger in another car started reviving his engine next to me. Egged on by the adrenaline and my foolish pride, I decided to show him what my car could do. The light turned green, I floored it, and the 442 took off, and in a flash I lost control of the car. The car spun out, skidded off the road and smashed into a telephone pole. The impact was severe, and the car actually rose up against the pole and rolled back. A transformer on the telephone pole detached and fell onto the hood of the 441 obliterating the engine. I lost consciousness. My friends were bruised and shaken. When I came to in the hospital, it was a day and a half later. The first thing I asked was *"Where is my wife?"* The doctor assured me she was okay and I called her.

The accident was a wake-up call. From that day on, I became a more cautious and deliberate driver. I rarely drank and drove. I don't speed for the thrill of it. I had seen the edge and had no intention of going over it again. Even when I later owned a Corvette, I treated it with respect, not trying the stunts I had with that 442. But what a machine she was! That crash took away my dream car, but it gave me something more important: perspective and value of life!

Years later, in 2015, another incident would again remind me of life's fragility. My wife, Janie, and I were visiting her mother in Hendersonville, North Carolina. We went out to eat at Red Lobster, and I indulged in lobster tails with drawn butter. It was a feast. Back at Janie's Mother's condo, I took all my regular medications, including lisinopril, and prepared for bed. I began to itch uncontrollably. It started as a minor irritation, then escalated into full-blown agony – similar to being covered from head to toe in poison ivy. We searched for Benadryl to no avail. I tried taking a shower, hoping the water would calm the burning itch, but it barely helped.

Janie looked at me with alarm, when I asked her what I should do next, and she realized I was unable to annunciate my words. She told me to put something on – _anything_ would be fine, we were going to the Emergency Room (which, since we were in Hendersonville, was less than 5 minutes away). I put on a pair of shorts, slippers and a t-shirt, barely coherent from the itching and swelling. At the ER, while Janie dealt with the security check, I tried to explain my symptoms to the nurse, but I couldn't talk anymore. I sat down, dizzy, overwhelmed, and then passed out. I would later learn I just fell into the wheelchair – just in time. Janie explained everything to the doctor on call. The ER doctor knew exactly what was happening: an allergic reaction – initially thought to be caused by the lobster, but 3 epi pens later it was determined to be the lisinopril. I had taken this drug for 7 years with no difficulty. Fortunately, she had seen this before and fortunately realized what it was from other patients she had treated. The doctor then intubated me, and sedated me. I woke up three days later, confused and disoriented.

The first thing I asked when I woke up was: *"Who won the Alabama football game?"* I didn't realize I had lost three entire days of my life. It was surreal. The calendar told me it was January 3rd. I thought it was still the 1st of January. That allergic reaction could have killed me if Janie had not taken prompt action and the ER doctor hadn't made her timely diagnosis and treatment. It took 2 other blood pressure medications to replace the lisinopril. That brush with death has stayed with me. I reminded me of how close we always are to the edge, and how important the right people, at the right time, can be.

But, life wasn't done testing me. Just 6 months later, on Memorial Day, I was visiting my son for the holiday. Right after dinner I began feeling strange and I found I was staggering. My son asked if I was okey and I said I didn't think so – he and his father-in-law managed to get me into his car and he drove me to the hospital in Franklin. Fortunately, the ER doctor went to work on me immediately and determined I had had a hemorrhagic stroke. They prepared to send me to Mission Hospital in Asheville. Somehow, they determined I didn't need to go by helicopter, but sent me in an ambulance – Janie met me there (she had been visiting her Mother). The recovery from this was slow and arduous, even now I have trouble with my memory, walking, and writing, but I persevere.

Then, in 2018, I had another mountain to climb – this time from my family. Thanks to my older brother, an orthopedic surgeon, my brothers and I had made a pact to get regular prostate exams. For years, my PSA levels were barely above zero. Then, in one year it jumped from 0.3 to 2.0. Not alarming, but worth watching. A year later, it had jumped from 2.0 to 6. That's when the doctor said: *"We need to have a biopsy."* The results came in: prostate cancer. Aggressive and fast-moving. Within two weeks, I was on the operating table. The cancer was spreading to part of my bladder, so he removed that portion, too. The surgeon told Janie it was a miracle we caught it when we did. A few more months, would have been too late.

I underwent weeks of radiation therapy following the surgery. It was grueling, but I never lost hope. I relied on my faith in the Lord, Janie's steadfast presence, and the wisdom of a very good doctor. The same optimism that helped me survive a car crash, an allergic reaction, and stroke got me through the cancer. Today, my PSA is zero.

What did I learn from these four life-threatening experiences? That life is both fragile and resilient. We're all more vulnerable than we like to admit. But also, with love, faith, and swift thinking, survival is possible. Each of these events, the car crash, the allergic reaction, the stroke and the cancer have changed me.

I've seen how quickly everything can change. One wrong turn, one pill, or unnoticed symptom can kill you. But I've also seen how strong the human spirit is, particularly when it is bolstered by faith, love, and a sense of purpose. Today, I live with a grateful heart, and I share these stories, not for sympathy, but in hope they'll help someone find Jesus. Pay attention, trust the Bible's message – Jesus is truly the only way, the essence of all that is true, and the only way to eternal life – no matter how winding and hard the road of life may get.

CHAPTER 10:

LEGACY AND REFLECTIONS

It was a quiet Sunday afternoon, and the house hummed with the soft rhythm of family life. The grandchildren had been running through the halls not long before, their laughter still lingering like the aroma of the fresh-baked cookies my wife had made that morning. I had just settled into my favorite chair, the one by the window with a phenomenal view of the mountains! The sunlight spilled through the glass, warming my knees, and I sat there thinking – not just about the day – but about the years. About what I hoped my family would remember when I'm no longer around sitting in that chair.

There comes a time in life when the present moment stretches back into memory and forward into legacy. For me, that time has come. If I could gather my children and grandchildren around this chair, if I could look each one in the eye and tell them what matters most before my time is up, it would be this: ***Never forget Jesus and what He did for us.*** ***Never trade truth for convenience – always choose love*** ***and care for others.***

I am not a perfect man. I've made mistake, some big, some small, and a few that still haunt me late at night. But God has been so good to me. Even when I took wrong turns, He was faithful and guided me back to where I needed to be. I hope my family will remember me, not for the times I've stumbled, but for the times I got back up because of God's help and guidance.

When I think about the legacy I want to leave, I don't think of wealth or achievements, I think of values. I want my grandchildren and their children to remember me as a man who loved God, loved his family, and did his best to live by the Bible. Church attendance wasn't always a good fit for me, I'll admit that, but I never stopped believing, and I ever stopped searching for knowledge to come closer to God. I wanted to show them that faith isn't about pretending to be flawless; it's about showing up with a heart willing to follow.

When grandchildren came to visit our home, we didn't skip church to entertain them. O, they came with us. We made it clear: if you're staying in our home, we worship together. Not because we're trying to be rigid, but because we wanted to model something real. Faith isn't something you put on like a Sunday suit. It' a way of life. You live it, day-in and day-out, through choices whether big or small.

One lesson I've tried to pass along is about honesty. You'll face moments in life where cutting corners looks easy – possibly better. When someone says: *"Just fudge the numbers a bit"*, or, *"No one will notice if you copy this."* I want my grandchildren to know that **God knows our deeds**. <u>**Nothing escapes his knowledge**</u>, regardless of how small or great. So be obedient to God – don't lie to anyone – just keep quiet. That lie will weigh heavily on your heart. So be honest – even when it's hard or not expeditious. If you can't tell the truth, then don't say anything at all. Silence is better than a lie.

I've always believed that how you treat people matters more than how they treat you. I try to live by this: if people are good to you, be good to them. If they're not good to you, forgive them and walk away. Life is too short to carry grudges. That doesn't mean you let yourself be mistreated. It means you choose peace over revenge. That's how I've tried to live. That's how Jesus taught me to live.

Looking back, I never thought I'd make it to eighty. There are so many moments when I thought: *"This might be it."* But, here I am – my wife and I are both turning 81 this July, and we celebrated our 56th wedding anniversary just this past May, in 2025. That's not a small thing to say the least. I'll tell you, it hasn't always been easy. Marriage is built on hard work, forgiveness, compromise and trust. But most of all, it's built on love of your spouse and love of God above all else. There are many times – too numerous to count – when we didn't agree. At times, we had to pray through tears, but we stuck together through it, because when you love someone, you fight for them. You don't walk away when there's trouble. It's vital to let God lead. God and God alone will give you the strength to make it through. There were years when I lost sight of that. At times, I thought I knew better than God. I married once before, and it didn't work, not because she was a bad person, but because I didn't seek the Lord's counsel. I made decisions based on emotion, not prayer. That's one of those regrets I carry with me. But even then, God was merciful. He gave me another chance. He gave me my wife of 56 years, the woman who has stood by me through every moment of the highs and lows of life. If I could go back and change anything, it would be to wait on God's timing in everything.

We've made some good memories, too. We've taken our grandchildren on special trips. We've been on tours with every one of our grandchildren. The youngest is still growing up, but, Lord willing, we'll take him on a trip when he's old enough. Those adventures aren't just for fun. They're about investing in them, about showing them who we are, about making deposits of love and laughter that they'll carry forever.

One of my friends and I recently reconnected. Working alongside him again has brought back something I thought I'd lost – a sense of youth, of purpose and strength. It's funny how physical work can heal the spirit. My aches and pains weren't as much about old age as they were inactivity before reconnecting with my friend David. I've been feeling better than I have for a long time, and I give God the glory for that. He's not done with me yet.

Still, I know my time will come. When the Lord will call me home to be with Him! When that day comes, I want to go in peace, knowing I did my best to follow His will. I'm not afraid of death, not because I think I've earned heaven, but because I trust the One who created it, Jesus is the only answer. I pray my family holds onto that truth with both hands.

I've also thought a lot about my parents, lately. If I could revisit any moment, I'd go back to the day my mother died and hug her one more time, tell her I love her more than anything. I wish I could have said more. But I'm grateful for the final words I shared with my Dad. I told him I loved him, and he said the same. That's how we parted. That's a gift I'll treasure until my last breath.

When I go home to be with the Lord, I hope this book finds its way into the hands of my great-grandchildren, maybe even great-great-grandchildren. I hop they'll read thee words and fee a connection to the man I was. Not perfect, but a faithful person of God. Not rich, not famous, but deeply blessed.

So here's my message to you, whoever you are reading this, whether it's decades from now or just next week: **Don't ignore God – or the gift He offers you in Jesus."** That's the one decision that matters more than all the others you might make. Eternity is real. Heaven and hell are real. Choose Jesus. Read your Bible and learn to trust Him. Trust His plan. The world will constantly distract you and try to pull you away with things that won't last – like money, fame, comfort. They all fade away, but God's love doesn't – it's forever.

You'll face hard times in life – that's a guarantee. But you don't have to face them alone. Faith isn't about being strong all the time. It's about knowing where your strength comes from. God will carry you when you can't walk. I've seen it again and again in my own life. Every scar has a story, and every story has God's grace and mercy in it somewhere. So, walk with integrity, love with courage – and forgive quickly. Don't forget to laugh, particularly with your family. That's what matters in the end.

When you think of me, I hope you'll smile. I hope you'll say: *"He was a good man. He loved life, but most of all He loved the Lord."* That's the legacy I want to leave!

EPILOGUE

I am 80 years old. I became the person I was never expected to be. Now that I am here, I'm learning that retirement comes with both its blessings and its challenges. Retirement is fun, but it isn't cheap. If I may pass along just one piece of wisdom to those still working, it would be this: save for retirement while you can – work hard while you can, invest in a 401K plan (or similar), and trust The Lord in every aspect of your life.

These days, I collect my Navy pension and my Social Security. I have taken my savings and invested - not in big corporations or faceless banks - but in Real Estate.

My wife and I spend most of our time at home in the mountains. We find comfort in the routines we are following, children, and grandchildren's visits, though they are rare – they lead very busy lives. We enjoy watching the birds flying outside our window, or enjoying breakfast together without rushing out the door. Every now and then we take trips to visit family. These visits mean everything to us. We are even talking about taking another cruise some day. That is still on the horizon, and if it's God's will – we'll see it through.

I also work with a real estate friend. I call it my retirement hustle. My buddy, David, whom I work with. We trust each other. He finds projects, and I help him bring them to completion. He gives me purpose. It keeps me sharp. It reminds me that even in retirement, you can still build something worthwhile.

Another thing I want to leave behind – it will be a truth that will live longer than this book and my own life: **Trust the Lord – keep your eyes on Him.**

This world will try to change you, and none of it will matter in the end. The **only** decision that matters is the decision to follow Jesus and make Him LORD of your life – "yes" or "no"

– it's up to you and how you walk with our Lord. Eternity is forever.

Treat others the way you would like to be treated. That's not just a proverb – it's a way of life. Help others where you are able. Give people your presence if they want it. There are so many people in this world who have les than you. No matter what your bank account says, sometimes the greatest gift you can give is your time, your encouragement, your faith.

Stay in fellowship with people and go to church. Be part of a community of believers that loves others and prays together. That is the kind of bond that will carry you, when life gets too heavy. It will remind you that you are never alone.

And don't forget to enjoy your life. Sit with a good friend and share stories and your life experiences. Take trips, even if they are just to the next town. Life isn't always about grand adventures (although sometimes it can be), sometimes it just about the little things.

So, if you're reading this, whether you are young or old, whether you are starting or winding down, remember this: *"You are not promised tomorrow."* Live today with grace. Love like it matters – because it does! ALWAYS put your trust in the Lord. He will never let you down – He will never leave you or forsake you.

That is what I believe. That is the life I have lived. That is the message I leave with you.

Thank you for letting me share my journey. May the Lord bless you and keep you, all the days of your life. **Amen (John 3:16)**